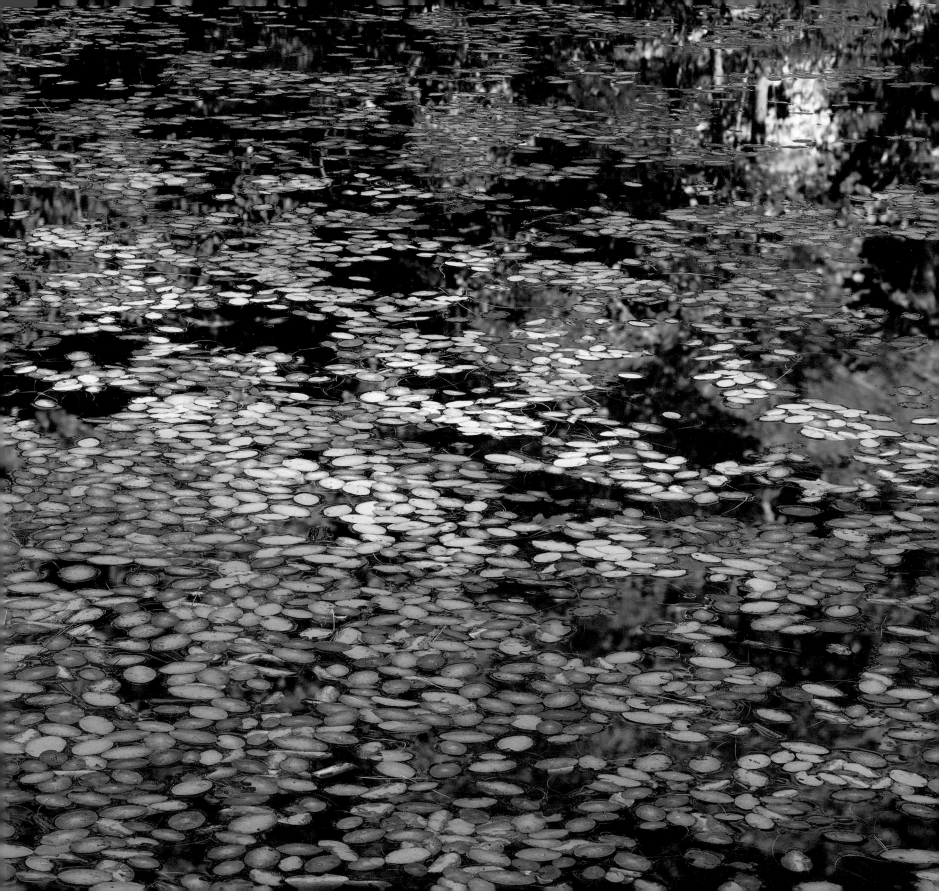

WALKING

An abridgement of the essay

by Henry David Thoreau

Photographs by John Wawrzonek

THE NATURE COMPANY

Berkeley, California

The Nature Company owes its vision to the world's great naturalists: Charles Darwin, Henry David Thoreau, John Muir, David Brower, Rachel Carson, Jacques Cousteau, and many others. Through their inspiration, we are dedicated to providing products and experiences which encourage the joyous observation, understanding, and appreciation of nature. We do not advocate, and will not allow to be sold in our stores, any products which result from the killing of wild animals for trophy purposes. Seashells, butterflies, furs, and mounted animal specimens fall into this category. Our goal is to provide you with products, insights, and experiences which kindle your own sense of wonder and which help you to feel good about yourself and the world in which you live.

Walking was prepared for publication at Marquand Books, Inc., Seattle
    Edited by Suzanne Kotz
    Designed by Ed Marquand

The Nature Company staff: Douglas Orloff, Catherine Kouts, Lori Largen, Anni Weston

Typesetting by Centerpoint Prepress Services, Seattle
Printed in Japan by Nissha Printing Co., Ltd.
Bound in the United States of America by Roswell Binding Co.

FOREWORD

HENRY DAVID THOREAU was born in Concord, Massachusetts, on July 12, 1817, and died there on May 6, 1862. With the exception of brief periods of absence during childhood and youth, excursions in adult years to the Maine woods, the White Mountains, Cape Cod, Quebec, and other localities, and one longer trip to Minnesota in 1861 in an effort to recover his health, Thoreau's whole life was spent within the borders of his native town. This was a distinction in which he rejoiced. "I cannot but regard it," he said, "as a kindness in those who have the steering of me that, by the want of pecuniary wealth, I have been nailed down to this my native region so long and steadily, and made to study and love this spot of earth more and more. What would signify in comparison a thin and diffused love and knowledge of the whole earth instead, got by wandering?"

Few men have ever lived who possessed so keen an appreciation of the wonders of the outdoor world, and few have been so thoroughly alive to the advantages of touring within one's native bounds: "I have travelled a great deal — in Concord." Day or night, through all the seasons, Thoreau explored Concord's fields, woods, and waterways. His travels were to some purpose. For the greater part of his life Thoreau kept a careful and extended record of his daily excursions and observations, accompanied by a multitude of moral and philosophical meditations, all written in a chaste and

picturesque style. His vocation was that of a writer — he had as many trades, he declared, as he had fingers. His studies embraced botany, zoology, and geology, and his writings combined the ethical, aesthetic, and scientific with the literary.

"Walking," like many of Thoreau's later natural history essays, began as a lecture, which he delivered many times during the 1850s. It was not published until 1863, in the *Atlantic Monthly*, and by then its author was dead. Thoreau's eloquent advocacy of the wild would become both cornerstone and inspiration for the twentieth-century movement to preserve wilderness areas.

Thoreau's thoughtful observations remind us that our understanding of the natural world depends on more than an appreciation of vast, majestic landscapes. Nature, when viewed up close, displays some of its finer lessons and rarer beauties. When we are patient and attentive, subtle delights effortlessly reveal themselves — in a walk through a grassy field, a stroll beside a riverbank, or even in a turn around one's own garden. There we witness the delicate facts of nature: dew suspended on a single blade, the unexpected path of a drifting leaf, the sudden appearance of a spring bloom.

The serenely beautiful images of photographer John Wawrzonek gently draw the eye to similar marvels in a countryside that pleasingly parallels Thoreau's. Musing on these quiet wonders, we sense how each part touches the whole and reflects, in microcosm, a likeness of the world.

WALKING

I WISH TO SPEAK A WORD FOR NATURE, for absolute freedom and wildness, as contrasted with a freedom and culture merely civil, — to regard man as an inhabitant, or a part and parcel of Nature, rather than a member of society. I wish to make an extreme statement, if so I may make an emphatic one, for there are enough champions of civilization: the minister and the school-committee, and every one of you will take care of that.

I HAVE MET WITH but one or two persons in the course of my life who understood the art of Walking, that is, of taking walks, — who had a genius, so to speak, for *sauntering*: which word is beautifully derived "from idle people who roved about the country, in the Middle Ages, and asked charity, under pretence of going *à la Sainte Terre*," to the Holy Land, till the children exclaimed, "There goes a Sainte-Terrer," a Saunterer, — a Holy-Lander. They who never go to the Holy Land in their walks, as they pretend, are indeed mere idlers and vagabonds; but they who do go there are saunterers in the good sense, such as I mean. Some, however, would derive the word from *sans terre*, without land or a home, which, therefore, in the good sense, will mean, having no particular home, but equally at home everywhere. For this is the secret of successful sauntering. He who sits still in a house all the time may be the greatest vagrant of all; but the saunterer, in the good sense, is no more vagrant than the meandering river, which is all the while sedulously seeking the shortest course to the sea. But I prefer the first, which, indeed, is the most probable derivation. For every walk is a sort of crusade, preached by some Peter the Hermit in us, to go forth and reconquer this Holy Land from the hands of the Infidels.

IT IS TRUE, WE ARE BUT faint-hearted crusaders, even the walkers, nowa-days, who undertake no persevering, never-ending enterprises. Our expeditions are but tours, and come round again at evening to the old hearth-side from which we set out. Half the walk is but retracing our steps. We should go forth on the shortest walk, perchance, in the spirit of undying adventure, never to return, — prepared to send back our embalmed hearts only as relics to our desolate kingdoms. If you are ready to leave father and mother, and brother and sister, and wife and child and friends, and never see them again, — if you have paid your debts, and made your will, and settled all your affairs, and are a free man, then you are ready for a walk.

To come down to my own experience, my companion and I, for I sometimes have a companion, take pleasure in fancying ourselves knights of a new, or rather an old, order, — not Equestrians or Chevaliers, not Ritters or riders, but Walkers, a still more ancient and honorable class, I trust. The chivalric and heroic spirit which once belonged to the Rider seems now to reside in, or perchance to have subsided into, the Walker, — not the Knight, but Walker Errant. He is a sort of fourth estate, outside of Church and State and People.

WE HAVE FELT THAT WE ALMOST alone hereabouts practised this noble art; though, to tell the truth, at least, if their own assertions are to be received, most of my townsmen would fain walk sometimes, as I do, but they cannot. No wealth can buy the requisite leisure, freedom, and independence, which are the capital in this profession. It comes only by the grace of God. It requires a direct dispensation from Heaven to become a walker. You must be born into the family of the Walkers. *Ambulator nascitur, non fit.* Some of my townsmen, it is true, can remember and have described to me some walks which they took ten years ago, in which they were so blessed as to lose themselves for half an hour in the woods; but I know very well that they have confined themselves to the highway ever since, whatever pretensions they may make to belong to this select class. No doubt they were elevated for a moment as by the reminiscence of a previous state of existence, when even they were foresters and outlaws.

. . . . .

I THINK THAT I CANNOT PRESERVE my health and spirits, unless I spend four hours a day at least, — and it is commonly more than that, — sauntering through the woods and over the hills and fields, absolutely free from all worldly engagements. You may safely say, A penny for your thoughts, or a thousand pounds. When sometimes I am reminded that the mechanics and shopkeepers stay in their shops not only all the forenoon, but all the afternoon too, sitting with crossed legs, so many of them, — as if the legs were made to sit upon, and not to stand or walk upon, — I think that they deserve some credit for not having all committed suicide long ago.

I, who cannot stay in my chamber for a single day without acquiring some rust, and when sometimes I have stolen forth for a walk at the eleventh hour of four o'clock in the afternoon, too late to redeem the day, when the shades of night were already beginning to be mingled with the daylight, have felt as if I had committed some sin to be atoned for, — I confess that I am astonished at the power of endurance, to say nothing of the moral insensibility, of my neighbors who confine themselves to shops and offices the whole day for weeks and months, ay, and years almost together. I know not what manner of stuff they are of, — sitting there now at three o'clock in the afternoon, as if it were three o'clock in the

morning. Bonaparte may talk of the three-o'clock-in-the-morning courage, but it is nothing to the courage which can sit down cheerfully at this hour in the afternoon over against one's self whom you have known all the morning, to starve out a garrison to whom you are bound by such strong ties of sympathy. I wonder that about this time, or say between four and five o'clock in the afternoon, too late for the morning papers and too early for the evening ones, there is not a general explosion heard up and down the street, scattering a legion of antiquated and house-bred notions and whims to the four winds for an airing, — and so the evil cure itself.

How womankind, who are confined to the house still more than men, stand it I do not know; but I have ground to suspect that most of them do not *stand* it at all. When, early in a summer afternoon, we have been shaking the dust of the village from the skirts of our garments, making haste past those houses with purely Doric or Gothic fronts, which have such an air of repose about them, my companion whispers that probably about these times their occupants are all gone to bed. Then it is that I appreciate the beauty and the glory of architecture, which itself never turns in, but forever stands out and erect, keeping watch over the slumberers.

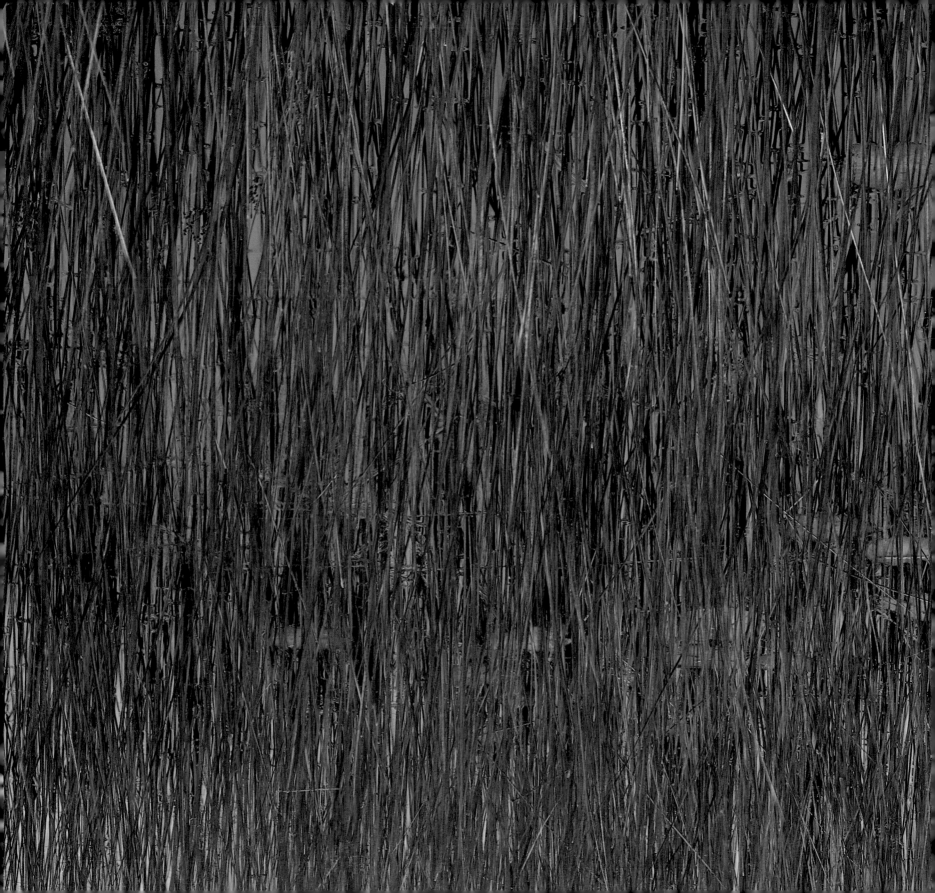

NO DOUBT TEMPERAMENT, AND, above all, age, have a good deal to do with it. As a man grows older, his ability to sit still and follow indoor occupations increases. He grows vespertinal in his habits as the evening of life approaches, till at last he comes forth only just before sundown, and gets all the walk that he requires in half an hour.

But the walking of which I speak has nothing in it akin to taking exercise, as it is called, as the sick take medicine at stated hours, — as the swinging of dumb-bells or chairs; but is itself the enterprise and adventure of the day. If you would get exercise, go in search of the springs of life. Think of a man's swinging dumb-bells for his health, when those springs are bubbling up in far-off pastures unsought by him!

Moreover, you must walk like a camel, which is said to be the only beast which ruminates when walking. When a traveller asked Wordsworth's servant to show him her master's study, she answered, "Here is his library, but his study is out of doors."

LIVING MUCH OUT OF DOORS, in the sun and wind, will no doubt produce a certain roughness of character, — will cause a thicker cuticle to grow over some of the finer qualities of our nature, as on the face and hands, or as severe manual labor robs the hands of some of their delicacy of touch. So staying in the house, on the other hand, may produce a softness and smoothness, not to say thinness of skin, accompanied by an increased sensibility to certain impressions. Perhaps we should be more susceptible to some influences important to our intellectual and moral growth, if the sun had shone and the wind blown on us a little less; and no doubt it is a nice matter to proportion rightly the thick and thin skin. But methinks that is a scurf that will fall off fast enough, — that the natural remedy is to be found in the proportion which the night bears to the day, the winter to the summer, thought to experience. There will be so much the more air and sunshine in our thoughts. The callous palms of the laborer are conversant with finer tissues of self-respect and heroism, whose touch thrills the heart, than the languid fingers of idleness. That is mere sentimentality that lies abed by day and thinks itself white, far from the tan and callus of experience.

WHEN WE WALK, WE NATURALLY go to the fields and woods: what would become of us, if we walked only in a garden or a mall? Even some sects of philosophers have felt the necessity of importing the woods to themselves, since they did not go to the woods. "They planted groves and walks of Platanes," where they took *subdiales ambulationes* in porticos open to the air. Of course it is of no use to direct our steps to the woods, if they do not carry us thither. I am alarmed when it happens that I have walked a mile into the woods bodily, without getting there in spirit. In my afternoon walk I would fain forget all my morning occupations and my obligations to society. But it sometimes happens that I cannot easily shake off the village. The thought of some work will run in my head, and I am not where my body is, — I am out of my senses. In my walks I would fain return to my senses. What business have I in the woods, if I am thinking of something out of the woods? I suspect myself, and cannot help a shudder, when I find myself so implicated even in what are called good works, — for this may sometimes happen.

MY VICINITY AFFORDS MANY good walks; and though for so many years I have walked almost every day, and sometimes for several days together, I have not yet exhausted them. An absolutely new prospect is a great happiness, and I can still get this any afternoon. Two or three hours' walking will carry me to as strange a country as I expect ever to see. A single farmhouse which I had not seen before is sometimes as good as the dominions of the King of Dahomey. There is in fact a sort of harmony discoverable between the capabilities of the landscape within a circle of ten miles' radius, or the limits of an afternoon walk, and the threescore years and ten of human life. It will never become quite familiar to you.

Nowadays almost all man's improvements, so called, as the building of houses, and the cutting down of the forest and of all large trees, simply deform the landscape, and make it more and more tame and cheap. A people who would begin by burning the fences and let the forest stand! I saw the fences half consumed, their ends lost in the middle of the prairie, and some worldly miser with a surveyor looking after his bounds, while heaven had taken place around him, and he did not see the angels going to and fro, but was looking for an old post-hole in the midst of paradise. I looked again, and saw him standing in the middle of a boggy, stygian fen, surrounded by devils, and he had found his bounds without a doubt, three little stones, where a stake had been driven, and looking nearer, I saw that the Prince of Darkness was his surveyor.

I CAN EASILY WALK TEN, fifteen, twenty, any number of miles, commencing at my own door, without going by any house, without crossing a road except where the fox and the mink do: first along by the river, and then the brook, and then the meadow and the woodside. There are square miles in my vicinity which have no inhabitant. From many a hill I can see civilization and the abodes of man afar. The farmers and their works are scarcely more obvious than woodchucks and their burrows. Man and his affairs, church and state and school, trade and commerce, and manufactures and agriculture, even politics, the most alarming of them all, — I am pleased to see how little space they occupy in the landscape. Politics is but a narrow field, and that still narrower highway yonder leads to it. I sometimes direct the traveller thither. If you would go to the political world, follow the great road, — follow that market-man, keep his dust in your eyes, and it will lead you straight to it; for it, too, has its place merely, and does not occupy all space. I pass from it as from a bean-field into the forest, and it is forgotten. In one half-hour I can walk off to some portion of the earth's surface where a man does not stand from one year's end to another, and there, consequently, politics are not, for they are but as the cigar-smoke of a man.

THE VILLAGE IS THE PLACE to which the roads tend, a sort of expansion of the highway, as a lake of a river. It is the body of which roads are the arms and legs, — a trivial or quadrivial place, the thoroughfare and ordinary of travellers. The word is from the Latin *villa*, which, together with *via*, a way, or more anciently *ved* and *vella*, Varro derives from *veho*, to carry, because the villa is the place to and from which things are carried. They who got their living by teaming were said *vellaturam facere*. Hence, too, apparently, the Latin word *vilis* and our vile; also *villain*. This suggests what kind of degeneracy villagers are liable to. They are wayworn by the travel that goes by and over them, without travelling themselves.

Some do not walk at all; others walk in the highways; a few walk across lots. Roads are made for horses and men of business. I do not travel in them much, comparatively, because I am not in a hurry to get to any tavern or grocery or livery-stable or depot to which they lead. I am a good horse to travel, but not from choice a roadster. The landscape-painter uses the figures of men to mark a road. He would not make that use of my figure. I walk out into a Nature such as the old prophets and poets, Menu, Moses, Homer, Chaucer, walked in. You may name it America, but it is not America: neither Americus Vespucius, nor Columbus, nor the rest were the discoverers of it. There is a truer account of it in mythology than in any history of America, so called, that I have seen.

· · · · ·

AT PRESENT, IN THIS VICINITY, the best part of the land is not private property; the landscape is not owned, and the walker enjoys comparative freedom. But possibly the day will come when it will be partitioned off into so-called pleasure-grounds, in which a few will take a narrow and exclusive pleasure only, — when fences shall be multiplied, and man-traps and other engines invented to confine men to the *public* road, and walking over the surface of God's earth shall be construed to mean trespassing on some gentleman's grounds. To enjoy a thing exclusively is commonly to exclude yourself from the true enjoyment of it. Let us improve our opportunities, then, before the evil days come.

What is it that makes it so hard sometimes to determine whither we will walk? I believe that there is a subtile magnetism in Nature, which, if we unconsciously yield to it, will direct us aright. It is not indifferent to us which way we walk. There is a right way; but we are very liable from heedlessness and stupidity to take the wrong one. We would fain take that walk, never yet taken by us through this actual world, which is perfectly symbolical of the path which we love to travel in the interior and ideal world; and sometimes, no doubt, we find it difficult to choose our direction, because it does not yet exist distinctly in our idea.

WHEN I GO OUT OF THE HOUSE for a walk, uncertain as yet whither I will bend my steps, and submit myself to my instinct to decide for me, I find, strange and whimsical as it may seem, that I finally and inevitably settle southwest, toward some particular wood or meadow or deserted pasture or hill in that direction. My needle is slow to settle, — varies a few degrees, and does not always point due southwest, it is true, and it has good authority for this variation, but it always settles between west and south-southwest. The future lies that way to me, and the earth seems more unexhausted and richer on that side. The outline which would bound my walks would be, not a circle, but a parabola, or rather like one of those cometary orbits which have been thought to be non-returning curves, in this case opening westward, in which my house occupies the place of the sun. I turn round and round irresolute sometimes for a quarter of an hour, until I decide, for a thousandth time, that I will walk into the southwest or west. Eastward I go only by force; but westward I go free. Thither no business leads me. It is hard for me to believe that I shall find fair landscapes or sufficient wildness and freedom behind the eastern horizon. I am not excited by the prospect of a walk thither; but I believe that the forest which I see in the western horizon stretches uninterruptedly toward the set-ting sun, and there are no towns nor cities in it of enough conse-quence to disturb me. Let me live where I will, on this side is the city, on that the wilderness, and ever I am leaving the city more and more, and withdrawing into the wilderness. I should not lay so much stress on this fact, if I did not believe that something like this is the prevailing tendency of my countrymen. I must walk toward Oregon, and not toward Europe. And that way the nation is moving, and I may say that mankind progress from east to west. Within a few years we have witnessed the phenomenon of a southeastward migration, in the settlement of Australia; but this affects us as a retrograde movement, and, judging from the moral and physical character of the first generation of Australians, has not yet proved a successful experiment. The eastern Tartars think that there is nothing west beyond Thibet. "The world ends there," say they, "beyond there is nothing but a shoreless sea." It is unmitigated East where they live.

We go eastward to realize history and study the world of art and literature, retracing the steps of the race; we go westward as into the future, with a spirit of enterprise and adventure. The Atlantic is a Lethean stream, in our passage over which we have had an opportunity to forget the Old World and its institutions. If we do not succeed this time, there is perhaps one more chance for the race left before it arrives on the banks of the Styx; and that is in the Lethe of the Pacific, which is three times as wide.

I KNOW NOT HOW SIGNIFICANT it is, or how far it is an evidence of sin-
gularity, that an individual should thus consent in his pettiest walk
with the general movement of the race; but I know that something
akin to the migratory instinct in birds and quadrupeds, — which, in
some instances, is known to have affected the squirrel tribe, impel-
ling them to a general and mysterious movement, in which they
were seen, say some, crossing the broadest rivers, each on its particular chip, with its tail raised for a sail, and bridging narrower
streams with their dead, — that something like the *furor* which
affects the domestic cattle in the spring, and which is referred to a
worm in their tails, — affects both nations and individuals, either
perennially or from time to time. Not a flock of wild geese cackles
over our town, but it to some extent unsettles the value of real
estate here, and, if I were a broker, I should probably take that
disturbance into account.

. . . . .

EVERY SUNSET WHICH I WITNESS inspires me with the desire to go to a West as distant and as fair as that into which the sun goes down. He appears to migrate westward daily, and tempt us to follow him. He is the Great Western Pioneer whom the nations follow. We dream all night of those mountain-ridges in the horizon, though they may be of vapor only, which were last gilded by his rays. The island of Atlantis, and the islands and gardens of the Hesperides, a sort of terrestrial paradise, appear to have been the Great West of the ancients, enveloped in mystery and poetry. Who has not seen in imagination, when looking into the sunset sky, the gardens of the Hesperides, and the foundation of all those fables?

Columbus felt the westward tendency more strongly than any before. He obeyed it, and found a New World for Castile and Leon. The herd of men in those days scented fresh pastures from afar.

· · · · ·

THE WEST OF WHICH I SPEAK is but another name for the Wild; and what I have been preparing to say is, that in Wildness is the preservation of the World. Every tree sends its fibres forth in search of the Wild. The cities import it at any price. Men plough and sail for it. From the forest and wilderness come the tonics and barks which brace mankind.

· · · · ·

HOPE AND THE FUTURE for me are not in lawns and cultivated fields, not in towns and cities, but in the impervious and quaking swamps. When, formerly, I have analyzed my partiality for some farm which I had contemplated purchasing, I have frequently found that I was attracted solely by a few square rods of impermeable and un-fathomable bog, — a natural sink in one corner of it. That was the jewel which dazzled me. I derive more of my subsistence from the swamps which surround my native town than from the culti-vated gardens in the village. There are no richer parterres to my eyes than the dense beds of dwarf andromeda (*Cassandra calyculata*) which cover these tender places on the earth's surface. Botany can-not go farther than tell me the names of the shrubs which grow there, — the high-blueberry, panicled andromeda, lamb-kill, azalea, and rhodora, — all standing in the quaking sphagnum. I often think that I should like to have my house front on this mass of dull red bushes, omitting other flower plots and borders, transplanted spruce and trim box, even gravelled walks, — to have this fertile spot under my windows, not a few imported barrow-fulls of soil only to cover the sand which was thrown out in digging the cellar. Why not put my house, my parlor, behind this plot, instead of behind that meagre assemblage of curiosities, that poor apology for a Nature and Art, which I call my front-yard? It is an effort to clear up and make a decent appearance when the carpenter and mason have departed, though done as much for the passer-by as the dweller within. The most tasteful front-yard fence was never an agreeable object of study to me; the most elaborate ornaments, acorn-tops, or what not, soon wearied and disgusted me. Bring your sills up to the very edge of the swamp, then, (though it may not be the best place for a dry cellar,) so that there be no access on that side to citizens. Front-yards are not made to walk in, but, at most, through, and you could go in the back way.

Yes, though you may think me perverse, if it were proposed to me to dwell in the neighborhood of the most beautiful garden that ever human art contrived, or else of a Dismal swamp, I should certainly decide for the swamp. How vain, then, have been all your labors, citizens, for me!

.   .   .   .   .

TO PRESERVE WILD ANIMALS implies generally the creation of a forest for them to dwell in or resort to. So it is with man. A hundred years ago they sold bark in our streets peeled from our own woods. In the very aspect of those primitive and rugged trees, there was, methinks, a tanning principle which hardened and consolidated the fibres of men's thoughts. Ah! already I shudder for these comparatively degenerate days of my native village, when you cannot collect a load of bark of good thickness, — and we no longer produce tar and turpentine.

The civilized nations — Greece, Rome, England — have been sustained by the primitive forests which anciently rotted where they stand. They survive as long as the soil is not exhausted. Alas for human culture! little is to be expected of a nation, when the vegetable mould is exhausted, and it is compelled to make manure of the bones of its fathers. There the poet sustains himself merely by his own superfluous fat, and the philosopher comes down on his marrow-bones.

· · · · ·

IN LITERATURE IT IS ONLY the wild that attracts us. Dulness is but
another name for tameness. It is the uncivilized free and wild
thinking in "Hamlet" and the "Iliad," in all the Scriptures and
Mythologies, not learned in the schools, that delights us. As the
wild duck is more swift and beautiful than the tame, so is the
wild — the mallard — thought, which 'mid falling dews wings its
way above the fens. A truly good book is something as natural,
and as unexpectedly and unaccountably fair and perfect, as a wild
flower discovered on the prairies of the West or in the jungles
of the East. Genius is a light which makes the darkness visible,
like the lightning's flash, which perchance shatters the temple
of knowledge itself, — and not a taper lighted at the hearth-stone
of the race, which pales before the light of common day.

English literature, from the days of the minstrels to the
Lake Poets, — Chaucer and Spenser and Milton, and even Shake-
speare, included, — breathes no quite fresh and in this sense wild
strain. It is an essentially tame and civilized literature, reflecting
Greece and Rome. Her wilderness is a green wood, — her wild man
a Robin Hood. There is plenty of genial love of Nature, but not
so much of Nature herself. Her chronicles inform us when her
wild animals, but not when the wild man in her, became extinct.

·   ·   ·   ·   ·

WHERE IS THE LITERATURE which gives expression to Nature? He would be a poet who could impress the winds and streams into his service, to speak for him; who nailed words to their primitive senses, as farmers drive down stakes in the spring, which the frost has heaved; who derived his words as often as he used them, — transplanted them to his page with earth adhering to their roots; whose words were so true and fresh and natural that they would appear to expand like the buds at the approach of spring, though they lay half-smothered between two musty leaves in a library, — ay, to bloom and bear fruit there, after their kind, annually, for the faithful reader, in sympathy with surrounding Nature.

·　·　·　·　·

THE WILDEST DREAMS OF WILD MEN, even, are not the less true, though they may not recommend themselves to the sense which is most common among Englishmen and Americans today. It is not every truth that recommends itself to the common sense. Nature has a place for the wild clematis as well as for the cabbage. Some expressions of truth are reminiscent, — others merely *sensible*, as the phrase is, — others prophetic. Some forms of disease, even, may prophesy forms of health. The geologist has discovered that the figures of serpents, griffins, flying dragons, and other fanciful embellishments of heraldry, have their prototypes in the forms of fossil species which were extinct before man was created, and hence "indicate a faint and shadowy knowledge of a previous state of organic existence." The Hindoos dreamed that the earth rested on an elephant, and the elephant on a tortoise, and the tortoise on a serpent; and though it may be an unimportant coincidence, it will not be out of place here to state, that a fossil tortoise has lately been discovered in Asia large enough to support an elephant. I confess that I am partial to these wild fancies, which transcend the order of time and development. They are the sublimest recreation of the intellect. The partridge loves peas, but not those that go with her into the pot.

IN SHORT, ALL GOOD THINGS are wild and free. There is something in a strain of music, whether produced by an instrument or by the human voice, — take the sound of a bugle in a summer night, for instance, — which by its wildness, to speak without satire, reminds me of the cries emitted by wild beasts in their native forests. It is so much of their wildness as I can understand. Give me for my friends and neighbors wild men, not tame ones. The wildness of the savage is but a faint symbol of the awful ferity with which good men and lovers meet.

I LOVE EVEN TO SEE THE domestic animals reassert their native rights, —
any evidence that they have not wholly lost their original wild
habits and vigor; as when my neighbor's cow breaks out of her pasture early in the spring and boldly swims the river, a cold, gray
tide, twenty-five or thirty rods wide, swollen by the melted snow.
It is the buffalo crossing the Mississippi. This exploit confers some
dignity on the herd in my eyes, — already dignified. The seeds of
instinct are preserved under the thick hides of cattle and horses,
like seeds in the bowels of the earth, an indefinite period.

Any sportiveness in cattle is unexpected. I saw one day a
herd of a dozen bullocks and cows running about and frisking in
unwieldly sport, like huge rats, even like kittens. They shook their
heads, raised their tails, and rushed up and down a hill, and I per-
ceived by their horns, as well as by their activity, their relation to
the deer tribe. But, alas! a sudden loud *Whoa!* would have damped
their ardor at once, reduced them from venison to beef, and stiff-
ened their sides and sinews like the locomotive. Who but the Evil
One has cried, "Whoa!" to mankind? Indeed, the life of cattle, like
that of many men, is but a sort of locomotiveness; they move a side
at a time, and man, by his machinery, is meeting the horse and the
ox half-way. Whatever part the whip has touched is thenceforth
palsied. Who would ever think of a *side* of any of the supple tribe,
as we speak of a *side* of beef?

I rejoice that horses and steers have to be broken before they can be made the slaves of men, and that men themselves have some wild oats still left to sow before they become submissive members of society. Undoubtedly, all men are not equally fit subjects for civilization; and because the majority, like dogs and sheep, are tame by inherited disposition, this is no reason why the others should have their natures broken that they may be reduced to the same level. Men are in the main alike, but they were made several in order that they might be various. If a low use is to be served, one man will do nearly or quite as well as another; if a high one, individual excellence is to be regarded. Any man can stop a hole to keep the wind away, but no other man could serve so rare a use as the author of this illustration did. Confucius says, — "The skins of the tiger and the leopard, when they are tanned, are as the skins of the dog and the sheep tanned." But it is not the part of a true culture to tame tigers, any more than it is to make sheep ferocious; and tanning their skins for shoes is not the best use to which they can be put.

. . . . .

HERE IS THIS VAST, SAVAGE, howling mother of ours, Nature, lying all around, with such beauty, and such affection for her children, as the leopard; and yet we are so early weaned from her breast to society, to that culture which is exclusively an interaction of man on man, — a sort of breeding in and in, which produces at most a merely English nobility, a civilization destined to have a speedy limit.

IN SOCIETY, IN THE BEST institutions of men, it is easy to detect a certain precocity. When we should still be growing children, we are already little men. Give me a culture which imports much muck from the meadows, and deepens the soil, — not that which trusts to heating manures, and improved implements and modes of culture only!

· · · · ·

I WOULD NOT HAVE EVERY MAN nor every part of a man cultivated, any more than I would have every acre of earth cultivated: part will be tillage, but the greater part will be meadow and forest, not only serving an immediate use, but preparing a mould against a distant future, by the annual decay of the vegetation which it supports.

. . . . .

WE HAVE HEARD OF A SOCIETY for the Diffusion of Useful Knowledge. It is said that knowledge is power; and the like. Methinks there is equal need of a Society for the Diffusion of Useful Ignorance, what we will call Beautiful Knowledge, a knowledge useful in a higher sense: for what is most of our boasted so-called knowledge but a conceit that we know something, which robs us of the advantage of our actual ignorance? What we call knowledge is often our positive ignorance; ignorance our negative knowledge. By long years of patient industry and reading of the newspapers, — for what are the libraries of science but files of newspapers? — a man accumulates a myriad facts, lays them up in his memory, and then when in some spring of his life he saunters abroad into the Great Fields of thought, he, as it were, goes to grass like a horse, and leaves all his harness behind in the stable. I would say to the Society of the Diffusion of Useful Knowledge, sometimes, — Go to grass. You have eaten hay long enough. The spring has come with its green crop. The very cows are driven to their country pastures before the end of May; though I have heard of one unnatural farmer who kept his cow in the barn and fed her on hay all the year round. So, frequently, the Society for the Diffusion of Useful Knowledge treats its cattle.

A MAN'S IGNORANCE SOMETIMES is not only useful, but beautiful, — while his knowledge, so called, is oftentimes worse than useless, besides being ugly. Which is the best man to deal with, — he who knows nothing about a subject, and, what is extremely rare, knows that he knows nothing, or he who really knows something about it, but thinks that he knows all?

My desire for knowledge is intermittent; but my desire to bathe my head in atmospheres unknown to my feet is perennial and constant. The highest that we can attain to is not Knowledge, but Sympathy with Intelligence. I do not know that this higher knowledge amounts to anything more definite than a novel and grand surprise on a sudden revelation of the insufficiency of all that we called Knowledge before, — a discovery that there are more things in heaven and earth than are dreamed of in our philosophy. It is the lighting up of the mist by the sun. Man cannot *know* in any higher sense than this, any more than he can look serenely and with impunity in the face of sun: "You will not perceive that, as perceiving a particular thing," say the Chaldean Oracles.

There is something servile in the habit of seeking after a law which we may obey. We may study the laws of matter at and for our convenience, but a successful life knows no law. It is an unfortunate discovery certainly, that of a law which binds us where we did not know before that we were bound.

.   .   .   .   .

IT IS REMARKABLE HOW FEW events or crises there are in our histories; how little exercised we have been in our minds; how few experiences we have had. I would fain be assured that I am growing apace and rankly, though my very growth disturb this dull equanimity, — though it be with struggle through long, dark, muggy nights or seasons of gloom. It would be well, if all our lives were a divine tragedy even, instead of this trivial comedy or farce. Dante, Bunyan, and others, appear to have been exercised in their minds more than we: they were subjected to a kind of culture such as our district schools and colleges do not contemplate. Even Mahomet, though many may scream at his name, had a good deal more to live for, ay, and to die for, than they have commonly.

When, at rare intervals, some thought visits one, as perchance he is walking on a railroad, then indeed the cars go by without his hearing them. But soon, by some inexorable law, our life goes by and the cars return.

. . . . .

WHILE ALMOST ALL MEN feel an attraction drawing them to society, few are attracted strongly to Nature. In their relation to Nature men appear to me for the most part, notwithstanding their arts, lower than the animals. It is not often a beautiful relation, as in the case of the animals. How little appreciation of the beauty of the landscape there is among us! We have to be told that the Greeks called the world Beauty, or Order, but we do not see clearly why they did so, and we esteem it at best only a curious philological fact.

FOR MY PART, I FEEL THAT with regard to Nature I live a sort of border life, on the confines of a world into which I make occasional and transional and transient forays only, and my patriotism and allegiance to the State into whose territories I seem to retreat are those of a moss-trooper. Unto a life which I call natural I would gladly follow even a will-o'-the-wisp through bogs and sloughs unimaginable, but no moon nor fire-fly has shown me the causeway to it. Nature is a personality so vast and universal that we have never seen one of her features. The walker in the familiar fields which stretch around my native town sometimes finds himself in another land than is described in their owners' deeds, as it were in some far-away field on the confines of the actual Concord, where her jurisdiction ceases, and the idea which the word Concord suggests ceases to be suggested. These farms which I have myself surveyed, these bounds which I have set up, appear dimly still as through a mist; but they have no chemistry to fix them; they fade from the surface of the glass; and the picture which the painter painted stands out dimly from beneath. The world with which we are commonly acquainted leaves no trace, and it will have no anniversary.

I TOOK A WALK ON SPAULDING'S FARM the other afternoon. I saw the setting sun lighting up the opposite side of a stately pine wood. Its golden rays straggled into the aisles of the wood as into some noble hall. I was impressed as if some ancient and altogether admirable and shining family had settled there in that part of the land called Concord, unknown to me. . . . I saw their park, their pleasure-ground, beyond through the wood, in Spaulding's cranberry-meadow. The pines furnished them with gables as they grew. Their house was not obvious to vision; the trees grew through it. I do not know whether I heard the sounds of a suppressed hilarity or not. They seemed to recline on the sunbeams. . . . The farmer's cart-path, which leads directly through their hall, does not in the least put them out, — as the muddy bottom of a pool is sometimes seen through the reflected skies. They never heard of Spaulding, and do not know that he is their neighbor, — notwithstanding I heard him whistle as he drove his team through the house. Nothing can equal the serenity of their lives. Their coat of arms is simply a lichen. I saw it painted on the pines and oaks. Their attics were in the tops of the trees. They are of no politics. There was no noise of labor. I did not perceive that they were weaving or spinning. Yet I did detect, when the wind lulled and hearing was done away, the finest imaginable sweet musical hum, — as of a distant hive in May, which perchance was the sound of their thinking. They had no idle thoughts, and no one without could see their work, for their industry was not as in knots and excrescences embayed.

·   ·   ·   ·   ·

WE HUG THE EARTH, — how rarely we mount! Methinks we might elevate ourselves a little more. We might climb a tree, at least. I found my account in climbing a tree once. It was a tall white pine, on the top of a hill; and though I got well pitched, I was well paid for it, for I discovered new mountains in the horizon which I had never seen before, — so much more of the earth and the heavens. I might have walked about the foot of the tree for threescore years and ten, and yet I certainly should never have seen them. But, above all, I discovered around me, — it was near the end of June, — on the ends of the topmost branches only, a few minute and delicate red cone-like blossoms, the fertile flower of the white pine looking heavenward. I carried straightway to the village the topmost spire, and showed it to stranger jurymen who walked the streets, — for it was court-week, — and to farmers and lumber-dealers and wood-choppers and hunters, and not one had ever seen the like before, but they wondered as at a star dropped down. Tell of ancient architects finishing their works on the tops of columns as perfectly as on the lower and more visible parts! Nature has from the first expanded the minute blossoms of the forest only toward the heavens, above men's heads and unobserved by them. We see only the flowers that are under our feet in the meadows. The pines have developed their delicate blossoms on the highest twigs of the wood every summer for ages, as well over the heads of Nature's red children as of her white ones; yet scarcely a farmer or hunter in the land has ever seen them.

ABOVE ALL, WE CANNOT AFFORD not to live in the present. He is blessed over all mortals who loses no moment of the passing life in remembering the past. Unless our philosophy hears the cock crow in every barn-yard within our horizon, it is belated. That sound commonly reminds us that we are growing rusty and antique in our employments and habits of thought. His philosophy comes down to a more recent time than ours. There is something suggested by it that is a newer testament, — the gospel according to this moment. He has not fallen astern; he has got up early, and kept up early, and to be where he is to be in season, in the foremost rank of time. It is an expression of the health and soundness of Nature, a brag for all the world, — healthiness as of a spring burst forth, a new fountain of the Muses, to celebrate this last instant of time. Where he lives no fugitive slave laws are passed. Who has not betrayed his master many times since last he heard that note?

The merit of this bird's strain is in its freedom from all plaintiveness. The singer can easily move us to tears or to laughter, but where is he who can excite in us a pure morning joy? When, in doleful dumps, breaking the awful stillness of our wooden sidewalk on a Sunday, or, perchance, a watcher in the house of mourning, I hear a cockerel crow far or near, I think to myself, "There is one of us well, at any rate," — and with a sudden gush return to my senses.

WE HAD A REMARKABLE SUNSET one day last November. I was walking in a meadow, the source of a small brook, when the sun at last, just before setting, after a cold gray day, reached a clear stratum in the horizon, and the softest, brightest morning sunlight fell on the dry grass and on the stems of the trees in the opposite horizon, and on the leaves of the shrub-oaks on the hill-side, while our shadows stretched long over the meadow eastward, as if we were the only motes in its beams. It was such a light as we could not have imagined a moment before, and the air also was so warm and serene that nothing was wanting to make a paradise of that meadow. When we reflected that this was not a solitary phenomenon, never to happen again, but that it would happen forever and ever an infinite number of evenings, and cheer and reassure the latest child that walked there, it was more glorious still.

THE SUN SETS ON SOME RETIRED meadow, where no house is visible, with all the glory and splendor that it lavishes on cities, and perchance, as it has never set before, — where there is but a solitary marsh-hawk to have his wings gilded by it, or only a musquash looks out from his cabin, and there is some little black-veined brook in the midst of the marsh, just beginning to meander, winding slowly round a decaying stump. We walked in so pure and bright a light, gilding the withered grass and leaves, so softly and serenely bright, I thought I had never bathed in such a golden flood, without a ripple or a murmur to it. The west side of every wood and rising ground gleamed like the boundary of Elysium, and the sun on our backs seemed like a gentle herdsman driving us home at evening.

So we saunter toward the Holy Land, till one day the sun shall shine more brightly than ever he has done, shall perchance shine into our minds and hearts, and light up our whole lives with a great awakening light, as warm and serene and golden as on a bank-side in autumn.

PHOTOGRAPHER'S STATEMENT

SINCE MY FIRST DAYS of photographing, some nineteen years ago, I have believed my subjects were in danger of disappearing, either because they went unnoticed or through simple neglect. Capturing these views on film, I thought, would help focus attention not only on the need to preserve natural areas but on the importance of planning our lives so we enjoy their beauty more.

When I revisit favorite sites, I see that photographs do not recur. A special combination of light, weather, and vegetation rarely happens twice. And in a few cases, the location has been paved over, the view has been lost behind trees grown taller, or the vegetation has been replaced by a new species.

One of my greatest surprises has been finding especially wonderful scenes in the most ordinary places. I had expected to make my photographs on mountaintops or in national parks, not on the interstate or in vacant lots. Even photographs I have made in famous parks (Baxter, Acadia, Walden) have been surprises, occurring in out-of-the-way places, underfoot, and at unexpected times. Many of them I could not have imagined. Most have come from a kind of "sauntering," a wandering in which I follow only my intuition.

The experience of finding nearby beauty came into better focus for me when I read *Ceremonial Time* by John Hanson Mitchell, a book about the place in Littleton, Massachusetts, where he lives.

Wilderness and wildlife, history, life itself, for that matter, is something that takes place somewhere else, it seems. You must travel to witness it, you must get in your car in summer and go off to look at things which some "expert". . . tells you is important, or beautiful, or historic. In spite of their admitted grandeur, I find such well-documented places somewhat boring. What I prefer . . . is that undiscovered country of the nearby, the secret world that lurks beyond the night windows and at the fringes of cultivated backyards.

This passage inspired me to write a short verse about these hidden worlds:

> Out of the corner of my eye,
> in the hidden world of the nearby,
> untended gardens thrive,
> or pass from time, unnoticed.

All of us must notice not just beauty itself but the effect upon our souls when we ignore and destroy it. It is much to our benefit to nourish and preserve the beauty of our natural world, just as it nourishes and preserves us.

John Wawrzonek
Southborough, Massachusetts
January 1993

LIST OF PHOTOGRAPHS

All the photographs were made with a 4-by-5-inch view camera. I carry a studio-type monorail camera, along with lenses, tripod, and film on a pack frame. Lenses are by Nikon, Schneider, and Rodenstock and are in focal lengths from 75mm to 300mm. The film is either Kodak Ektachrome 64, Fuji Velvia, or Polaroid Professional Chrome 100. I prefer to make large prints (up to 32 by 40 inches) to reveal texture and to produce a sense of envelopment when the image is viewed closely. I use the Kodak dye-transfer process or the UltraStable carbon-pigment process, both of which offer the control and color quality necessary to reproduce the colors that I see. — J.W.

Page 1.   **LILY POND WITH REFLECTIONS,** October 1991, Walden Pond State Reservation, Concord, Massachusetts.

Page 3.   **BLUEBERRIES IN A STONY FIELD,** October 1989, near Ellsworth, Maine.

Page 4.   **MEADOW OF FERNS,** July 1979, Hopkinton State Park, Hopkinton, Massachusetts.

Page 8.   **RAIN TO LEAF TO ROCK,** May 1987, Hopkinton State Park, Hopkinton, Massachusetts.

Page 10.   **MAPLE LEAVES AND TALL GRASS,** October 1988, Interstate 90, Millbury, Massachusetts.

Page 13.   **BEECH, MAPLE, AND BIRCH TREES,** October 1992, White Mountains National Forest, New Hampshire.

Page 15.   **BLUEBERRIES,** September 1990, Cherryfield, Maine.

Page 16.   **TIDAL MARSH,** September 1992, Route 3, Bar Harbour, Maine.

Page 19.   **BLUEBERRY, BARK, AND LICHENS,** October 1991, near Walden Pond, Lincoln, Massachusetts.

Page 21.   **SINGULAR LUMINARY,** October 1988, Baxter State Park, Maine.

Page 22.   **REEDS IN A POND,** October 1990, Acadia National Park, Maine.

Page 24.   **MAPLE TREES IN FLOWER AND RIVER-BANK,** May 1991, Sudbury River, Ashland, Massachusetts.

Page 27.   **SALT HAY,** July 1991, Route 533, near Beaver Dam, New Jersey.

Page 29.   **FERNS WITH FROST AT SUNRISE,** October 1977, Cambridge, Vermont.

Page 30.   **FLOWERING MAPLE TREES ON A FOGGY MORNING,** April 1991, Interstate 90, Weston, Massachusetts.

Page 32.   **WILD LEAF AND FLOWER,** October 1988, Cummington, Massachusetts.

Page 35.   **OVERLOOK AFTER STORM,** November 1990, Quabbin Reservoir, Ware, Massachusetts.

Page 37.   **RIVER VALLEY AFTER STORM,** May 1989, Quinapoxet River, Interstate 190, Holden, Massachusetts.

Page 38.   **LAST SNOW,** March 1992, Walden Pond, Walden Pond State Reservation, Concord, Massachusetts.

Page 41.   **LEAVES AND LIGHT ON BLACK WATER,** October 1985, Interstate 90, Millbury, Massachusetts.

Page 45.   **VIEW FROM LEDGES TRAIL,** October 1989, Baxter State Park, Maine.

Page 47.   **AUTUMN DAWN,** October 1991, Sudbury River, Ashland, Massachusetts.

Page 49.   **BLUEBERRY FIELDS AT SUNSET,** October 1991, Ellsworth, Maine.

Page 50. **SMALL MAPLE TREE,** October 1979, Stowe, Vermont.

Page 53. **CATTAILS AND SALT MARSH,** September 1990, near Crane Beach, Ipswich, Massachusetts.

Page 56. **WET LEAVES AND PINE NEEDLES,** October 1979, Upton State Forest, Upton, Massachusetts.

Page 59. **WATER-SHIELDS AND SKY REFLECTIONS,** October 1991, Walden Pond State Reservation, Concord, Massachusetts.

Page 60. **LAST GLOW ON A SPUR ROAD,** October 1988, Baxter State Park, Maine.

Page 63. **ROADSIDE,** May 1992, Interstate 90, Ludlow, Massachusetts.

Page 64. **REEDS, WIND, AND WATER,** October 1990, Acadia National Park, Maine.

Page 66. **ICE STORM III,** March 1985, Woodland Road, Southborough, Massachusetts.

Page 68. **REEDS AND REFLECTIONS,** October 1990, Acadia National Park, Maine.

Page 70. **GOLDENPERT, DRY EDGE OF SHALLOW POND,** July 1991, Brigantine National Wildlife Refuge, New Jersey.

Page 73. **ROOTS AND PINE NEEDLES,** April 1991, Walden Pond State Reservation, Concord, Massachusetts.

Page 75. **PATH WITH LEAVES AND FERNS,** October 1992, Sudbury River, Ashland, Massachusetts.

Page 76. **SALT MARSH GRASS,** October 1983, near Crane Beach, Ipswich, Massachusetts.

Page 79. **LAST ICE,** April 1992, Walden Pond State Reservation, Concord, Massachusetts.

Page 80. **ASPEN, MAPLE, AND BIRCH TREES,** October 1992, White Mountains National Forest, New Hampshire.

Page 83. **PICKERELWEED AND STARWORT,** July 1992, Landham Brook, Landham Road, Sudbury, Massachusetts.

Page 84. **SPRING SUNRISE,** May 1983, Exit 11, Interstate 90, Millbury, Massachusetts.

Page 87. **FROST, SHADOW, AND LIGHT,** October 1984, Route 85, Southborough, Massachusetts.

Page 89. **EARLY SPRING,** April 1992, Walden Pond State Reservation, Concord, Massachusetts.

Page 90. **AFTER ICE STORM,** December 1991, Sudbury River, Southborough, Massachusetts.

Page 93. **MONET'S MEADOW,** September 1981, Woodland Road, Southborough, Massachusetts.

Page 95. **WILD BLUEBERRIES AT SUNSET,** October 1991, Ellsworth, Maine.

Page 97. **WATER-SHIELDS IN SPRINGTIME,** May 1992, Walden Pond State Reservation, Concord, Massachusetts.

Page 98. **SPRING SUNRISE III,** May 1985, Exit 11, Interstate 90, Millbury, Massachusetts.

Page 101. **LICHENS AND TEABERRY LEAVES,** September 1990, Acadia National Park, Maine.

Page 102. **MAPLE TREES AND FIRST SNOW,** October 1988, Smuggler's Notch, Stowe, Vermont.

Page 105. **ROADSIDE MEADOW,** July 1992, Interstate 90, Framingham, Massachusetts.

Page 106. **LOOSESTRIFE,** July 1987, Cordaville Road, Ashland, Massachusetts.

Page 109. **VERNAL POOL,** June 1991, Walden Pond State Reservation, Concord, Massachusetts.

Page 110. **BIRCH, MAPLE, AND BEECH TREES,** October 1992, White Mountains National Forest, New Hampshire.

Page 112. **INDIGO BUSH,** June 1987, Beaver Brook, Beaver Brook Road, Littleton, Massachusetts.

Page 115. **DREAMED BROOK,** July 1987, Beaver Brook, Interstate 495, Littleton, Massachusetts.

ABOUT THE PHOTOGRAPHER

JOHN WAWRZONEK graduated from the Massachusetts Institute of Technology with S.B., M.S., and E.E. degrees in electrical engineering. He began photographing while working in engineering and marketing at Bose Corporation in Framingham, Massachusetts. Largely self-taught in photography, Wawrzonek studied briefly with Bela Kalman, Lauren Shaw, and Stephen Gersh. Wawrzonek now operates his own gallery and fine-art printing company in Worcester, Massachusetts. He resides with his wife in Southborough, Massachusetts.